the PAN'INO

maria teresa di marco   alessandro frassica

the PAN'INO

photographs by maurizio maurizi

Guido Tommasi Editore

table of contents

introduction

What could be more simple than a *panino*? Take some bread and butter, slice through the middle and fill it with whatever you like. Seen like this, the sandwich is almost an ''anti-cuisine'', a nomadic short-cut that allows for speed but little thought about what is on the plate.

When Alessandro Frassica thinks about his own Pan'ino, he considers it in a different way, not as a short-cut, but as a means of telling stories, creating layers of tales right there between the bread and butter. Because the sandwich may be simple, but not necessarily so easy to create.

It is a question of pure ingredients, people and choices. The quality of the product depends on various elements: pecorino cheese depends on the type of milk used; traditional mortadella of Bologna depends on the type of cooking and the wood-burning oven used, and mozzarella di bufala could have one of a hundred different meanings. Small, wonderful gems of pink salami or mortadella di Prato that are now all but extinct, preserves from Benevento, gorgonzola refiners from Verbania, Cetara anchovies, the invention of carciuga, the aroma of smoked caciocavallo cheese...

these are rich of such incalculable value that you have to go and look for them following both your nose and your brain.

You don't need hundreds of ingredients, even though variety means you'll never get bored, but have a good selection that you can count on so that you can have fun playing with different combinations, textures and temperatures.

A pan'ino is never random: savoury must be complemented by sweet, and strength accompanied by softness. The bitterness of turnip tops blends with the richness of mortadella, but also with the sumptuous consistency of salted cod's liver. Playing with flavours that interact with each other, sometimes in a most unexpected way, but always following the refined logic that infuses every recipe's process. If you have gorgonzola and anchovies together, or mortadella with truffle sauce between two slices of special bread, you'll have so much more than the algebraic sum of one and the other. It's true to say that in the kitchen one plus one really makes three.

'Ino is the actual place where all of this has happened every day, seven days a week, since 2006, in via dei Georgofili in the heart of Florence.
This book wishes to recount and demonstrate the simple magic of a very special place through its panini and through the faces of the people who eat and love them.

1. Choose your bread carefully: it holds all the ingredients together and above all, is the very substance of your panino.

2. To warm your bread, use a simple gas or electric oven (even a toaster oven): do not use microwave ovens or griddle pans.

3. Warm the bread for just a few minutes at medium temperature (140-160°C/250°-315°F): the bread must not dry out and the ingredients must not cook!

4. If the bread is too damp, proceed in two steps: first warm the open bread and then warm the filled panino.

5. Remember that temperature and texture are two fundamental elements of the panino.

6. Pay more attention to the thickness of the ingredients you use to fill your panino, not the weight: the idea is to make it easy to bite into, it must be pleasurable and substantial, not tiring!

7. Don't use ingredients straight from the fridge. It isn't nice to sink your teeth into a warm panino and then find the inside of it cold.

instructions for use

8. When using ingredients such as turnip tops or artichokes, it's always a good idea to chop them finely before putting them in the sandwich.

9. When you put your panino together, be careful not to leave ingredients hanging out of the bread, especially before putting it in the oven: during cooking, they will leak out of the bread, go all over the panino and above all, dirty the oven creating an unpleasant smell of burning.

10. Sauces are very important: they moisten the bread, bind the ingredients, make the taste more complex and provide vegetable elements that would otherwise be difficult to include.

11. You don't need a thousand ingredients: just choose top quality ingredients with care.

12. Feel free to experiment but remember that you must balance the flavours and create harmony with them.

13. In general, don't use more than 3 ingredients for one panino because it will be difficult to balance the result.

PANE AMORE & FANTASIA
(PANINO A NOSTRA SCELTA...) 8,00 €

I semplici
- MORTADELLA di BOLOGNA (Pasquini) 5,00 €
- SALAME TOSCANO 5,00 €
- FINOCCHIONA 5,00 €
- PROSCIUTTO TOSCANO 6,00 €
- BURRO e ACCIUGHE 6,00 €
- SCAMORZA e POMODORO 7,00 €
- SCAMORZA e ACCIUGHE 8,00 €
- SOPRASSATA DI GAVIGLIO 7,00

I nostri classici

con TAPENADE (pestato di OLIVE NERE al FORNO e PESCE AZZURRO)
- il SOLITO (prosciutto crudo, Tapenade, pecorino, pomodori) 8,00 €
- PECORINO al PESTO, TAPENADE e PORTODORI SECCHI 8,00 €
- PEPERONI alla GRIGLIA, TAPENADE e ACCIUGHE 8,00 €

con CARCIUGA (paté di CARCIOFI e ACCIUGHE)
- PECORINO e CARCIUGA 8,00 €
- SALAME ROSA e CARCIUGA 8,00 €

con PESTATO ZUCCHINE e ZAFFERANO
- SCAMORZA e PESTATO ZUCCHINE e ZAFFERANO 8,00 €
- SALAME ROSA e PESTATO ZUCCHINE e ZAFFERANO 8,00 €

Le specialità

con GORGONZOLA
- GORGONZOLA e ACCIUGHE 8,00 €
- GORGONZOLA e N'DUJA 8,00 €
- GORGONZOLA e MOSTARDA 8,00 €

con SALAME ROSA
- SALAME ROSA e CREMA di PARMIGIANO 8,00 €
- SALAME ROSA e PECORINO allo ZAFFERANO 8,00 €
- SALAME ROSA, SCAMORZA e MELANZANE 8,00 €
- SALAME ROSA CACIOCAVALLO AFFUMICATO 8,00 € 8,00 €
- FABIEN (SALAME ROSA, C.OBIOLA e MOSTARDA di PEPERONI)

con MORTADELLA
- MORTADELLA e PECORINO al PISTACCHIO 8,00 €
- MORTADELLA e CACIOCAVALLO AFFUMICATO 8,00 €

classics

THE USUAL

TUSCAN CURED HAM

FRESH PECORINO CHEESE BABY PLUM TOMATOES AND TAPENADE

This is an absolute winner, the first panino to be invented and realised starting from and reinterpreting the most classic of all classics: ham and cheese.
4 ingredients have been chosen (5 if we include the extra-virgin olive oil) so as to create a more complex harmony than usual: the full flavour of Tuscan cured ham, the sweetness of the pecorino, the bitter taste of the olives compensated by the fish and capers together with the slightly acidic freshness of the tomato. Nothing more, nothing less.

50 g/2 oz Tuscan cured ham from Casentino (matured 24 months)
1 slice (approx. 0.5cm/0.2") fresh sweet Seggiano pecorino cheese
1 heaped dessertspoon tapenade
2 baby plum, or small authentic San Marzano, tomatoes
A drizzle of extra-virgin olive oil

Cut the bread in half, warm it up then spread the tapenade on one half. Top with the sliced cured ham and the slice of pecorino cheese. Finish by adding the baby plum tomatoes and a drizzle of extra-virgin olive oil, then close.

MICHELE

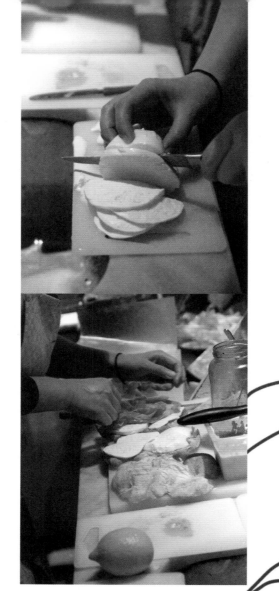

TUSCAN CURED HAM

MOZZARELLA CHEESE

50 g/2 oz Tuscan cured ham from Casentino (matured 24 months)
2 slices of buffalo mozzarella cheese from Paestum

Cut the bread in half and warm it briefly without drying it out. Fill it with 2 slices of mozzarella about 2cm/0.8" thick, then top with the machine-sliced cured ham and close.

If you can, use large mozzarella pieces (500g/4oz, or at least 250g/10oz). It is preferable to keep it in a cool, dry place, not the fridge, covered with its own whey.
It is one of the most classic and practical combinations; this must be why it's so popular. You can't go wrong, provided that you choose excellent ingredients.

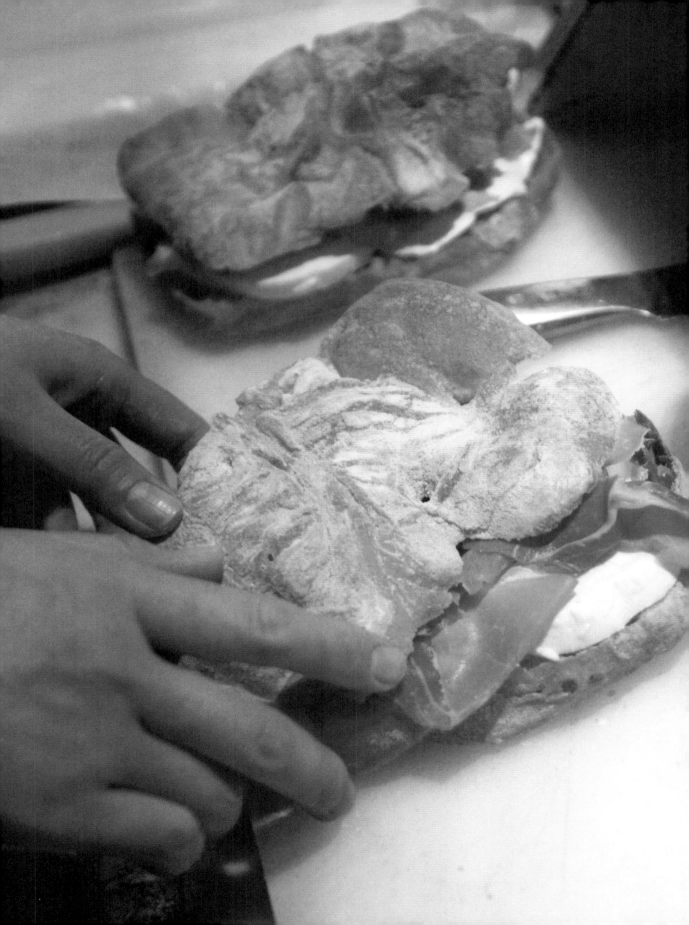

50 g/2 oz Tuscan cured ham from Casentino (matured for 24 months)
2 carciofi alla cafona (see p. 138)

TUSCAN CURED HAM

CARCIOFI ALLA CAFONA

Cut the bread in half, warm it for a few minutes then fill with the well-drained artichokes that have been cut into large slices so as to preserve their crunchiness. Top with the machine-sliced cured ham then close.

The special crunchiness and flavour of these artichokes go well with the richness of the cured ham in terms of both texture and sweetness.

50 g/2 oz Tuscan salami
1 good slice of scamorza cheese
3-4 slices of eggplant in olive oil
(preferably from Benevento)

Cut the bread in half, place the scamorza slice on one half and pop in the oven for a few minutes, just enough time for the cheese to soften without cooking. Remove from the oven and add the hand-cut salami then the eggplant, closing with the other slice of bread (the eggplant oil is then absorbed by the top half of the bread).

Tuscan salami calls for pecorino; using the scamorza creates a surprising aroma of cow's milk. Eggplant from Benevento lends a soft texture without tainting the mouth with too much vinegar.

TUSCAN SALAMI

SCAMORZA CHEESE AND EGGPLANT

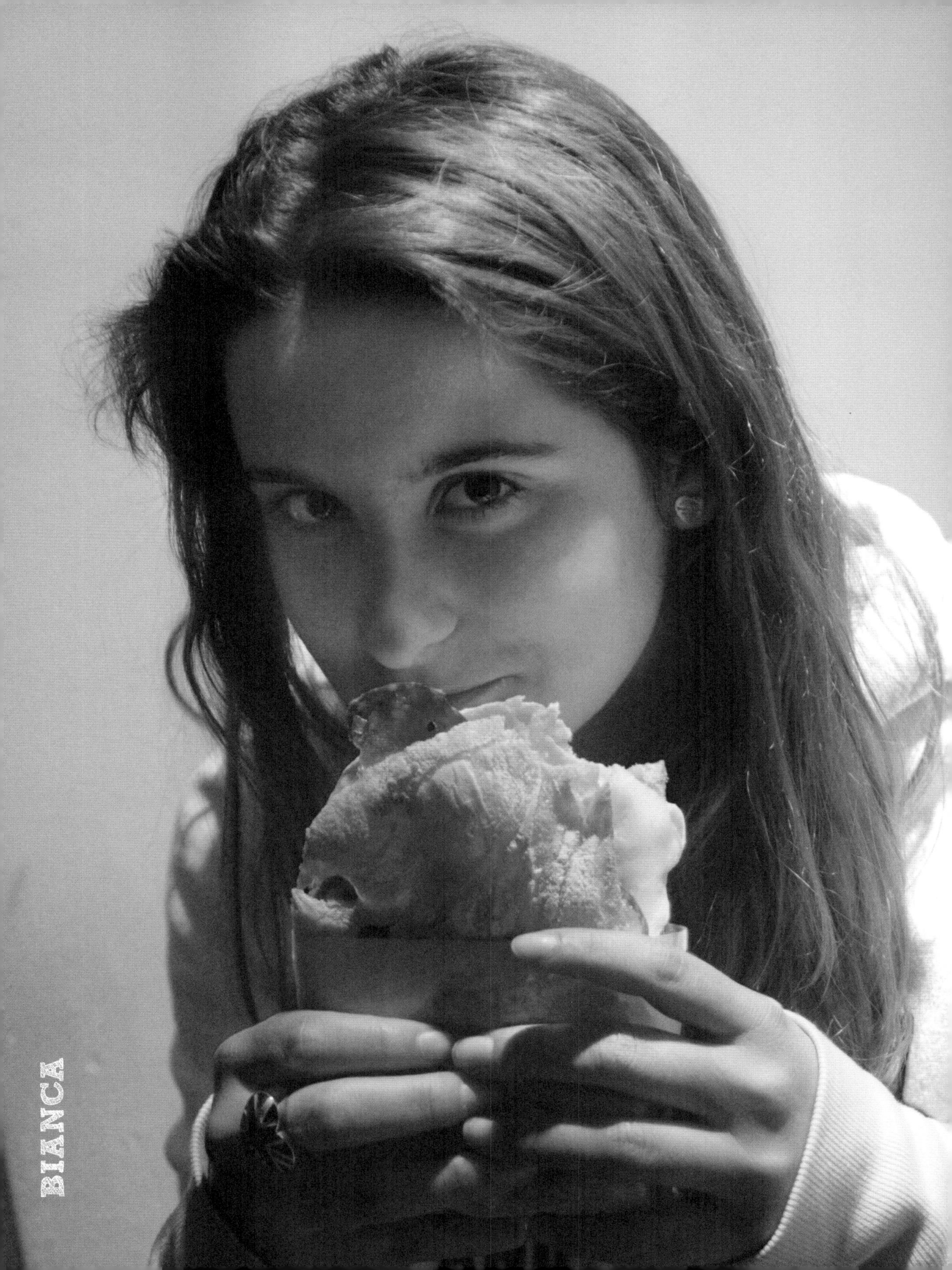

BIANCA

TUSCAN SALAMI

ANCHOVIES AND TRUFFLE SAUCE

50 g/2 oz Tuscan salami
3-4 slices of Cetara anchovies
1 dessertspoon truffle sauce

Divide the bread into two halves, warm them both, then spread the truffle sauce on one half, adding the anchovies and topping with the salami.

Anchovies and truffles work extremely well together. From this initial combination, we decided to go one step further by introducing salami. It shakes up the balance in terms of both taste and texture.

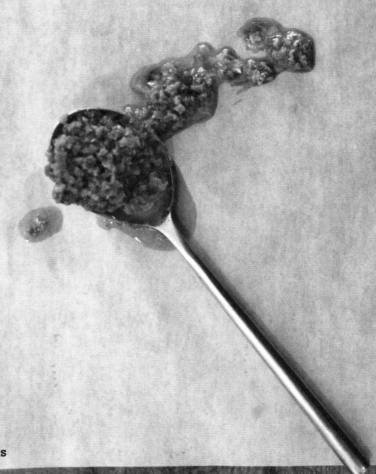

SILVIA

50 g/2 oz thinly sliced traditional Bologna mortadella
2 slices (about 0.5cm/0.2") pecorino cheese with pistachio nuts

Cut the bread in half, place the pecorino (cut into 2 slices for it to soften better) on one half and warm for 3 minutes at 150°C/300°F; be sure the cheese does not cook. Remove from the oven, top with the mortadella slices and close.

MORTADELLA

PECORINO CHEESE WITH PISTACHIO NUTS

In the true traditional Bolognese mortadella, which very few producers still cook in old wood-burning stoves, pistachio nuts would just not be right!
This is remedied in the form of a fresh Tuscan pecorino cheese to which a generous handful of Bronte pistachio nuts has been added.

PAN DI RAMERINO

MORTADELLA

50 g/2 oz thinly sliced traditional Bologna mortadella
1 pan di ramerino (see p. 163)

Cut the bread in half, open and warm it slightly, then place the mortadella inside. If you have the opportunity and you want to go overboard, you can make the bread yourself. As soon as it comes out of the oven, fill it with mortadella.

This recipe plays with flavours, using a sweet bread that in Tuscany, especially Florence, you can find in bakers' shops at springtime (traditionally on Maundy Thursday) with a delicious savoury touch of mortadella. This recipe needs nothing more.

ELISABETTA

MORTADELLA

GORGONZOLA AND PEPPER MUSTARD

**40 g/just under 1.5 oz thinly sliced traditional
    Bologna mortadella
1 scoop gorgonzola cheese (about 50g/2 oz)
1 dessertspoon pepper mustard**

Cut the bread roll in half, spread one half with gorgonzola and put in the oven for about 3 minutes. As soon as you remove the roll from the oven, add the mortadella and top with the pepper mustard (ideally using a squeezable tube for even spreading).

There has always been a very popular version using gorgonzola and pepper mustard on 'ino's menu, then the "chef next door" thought about adding mortadella to his own personal version.

NB Marco (Stabile) has his restaurant L'ora d'Aria right next door to 'ino.

MARCO

MORTADELLA

TRUFFLE SAUCE

60 g/just over 2 oz thinly sliced traditional Bologna mortadella
1 dessertspoon truffle sauce

Cut the roll and warm the two halves for a few minutes. Spread one half with the truffle sauce and place the fine machine-sliced mortadella on the other. Close.

The aroma of truffle is very intense so there's no need to exaggerate; it should be pleasant without becoming invasive. The aim is to find perfect harmony based on balance: in this case, the richness of the mortadella and the pronounced nature of the truffle.

CARLOTTA

MORTADELLA

FRESH ROBIOLA CHEESE AND TURNIP TOPS

50 g/2 oz thinly sliced traditional Bologna
    mortadella
1 dessertspoon fresh robiola cheese
2 dessertspoons turnip tops

Cut the bread roll in half, warm it and spread
one half with robiola. Add the finely chopped
turnip tops (lightly pan-fried with extra-virgin
olive oil, garlic and chili peppers as desired).
Top with mortadella and close.

*Here, the robiola with its neutral yet slightly
acidic taste plays an important role in combining
the bitterness of the turnip tops with the
richness of the mortadella. Vegetables, salami
and milk.*

GIUSEPPE

50 g/2 oz thinly sliced traditional Bologna mortadella
50 g/2 oz smoked caciocavallo cheese

Cut the ciabatta roll in two halves. Place the (not too thick) slices of caciocavallo cheese on one half and warm it all in the oven for a few minutes.
Once out of the oven, add the machine-sliced mortadella and close.

This combination goes much further than the usual panino with mortadella; this wonderful cheese really stands out in terms of both taste and texture.

MORTADELLA

SMOKED CACIOCAVALLO CHEESE

GIULIA

MORTADELLA

RED COW PARMESAN AND BALSAMIC VINEGAR

50 g/2 oz finely sliced traditional Bologna mortadella
50 g/2 oz Red Cow Parmesan cheese (matured 24 months)
1 dessertspoon Modena or high quality Reggio Emilia balsamic vinegar

Cut the bread roll and warm it for a minute or two without drying it out. First, place a layer of medium sized parmesan shavings on one half, then add the balsamic vinegar and top with the finely machine-sliced mortadella.

This panino is a sort of tribute to the region of Emilia Romagna, a kind of souvenir of travels marked by the discovery of the traditional and virtuous combination of Red Cow parmesan with balsamic vinegar. The mortadella rounds off the experience beautifully.

MORTADELLA

RICOTTA CHEESE AND CAPERS

ALESSANDRO

50 g/2 oz finely sliced classic Bologna mortadella
2 dessertspoons sheep's ricotta cheese
1 dessertspoon Pantelleria capers, with salt removed

Cut the bread roll and warm both halves in the oven for a few minutes. Spread one half with the ricotta, place the machine-sliced mortadella on the top and add the capers. Close.

Another Alessandro who loves 'ino invented this panino. This recipe shows how the introduction of just one miniscule ingredient can change a panino.
The capers are from Pantelleria, rigorously salted. The smaller they are the more pronounced is their aroma, so don't choose any larger than Lilliputian-sized.

MORTADELLA
PARMESAN CREAM

50 g/2 oz classic Bologna
    mortadella
2 dessertspoons Parmesan
    Cream

Cut the bread roll in two halves.
Spread the Parmesan Cream
on one half and put everything
in the oven for a few minutes
to soften the cheese without
cooking it. Once out of the oven,
add the mortadella and close
the panino.

*This is a great solution for Mums
in a pickle; this panino can make
any child eat healthily. It shows
just how it is possible to tickle
the fancy of any child's tastes,
weaning them off a banal ham
and cheese slice sandwich
forever with a very similar
variation. A historical classic of
'ino that uses pink salami instead
of mortadella is even closer to
this version.*

FABIEN

PINK SALAMI

GOAT'S CHEESE PEPPER MUSTARD

50 g/2 oz thinly sliced pink salami
50 g/2 oz fresh spreadable goat's cheese
1 dessertspoon pepper mustard

Cut the bread roll in half, warm it for a few minutes, spread one half with the goat's cheese, cover with the pepper mustard and top with the slices of pink salami.

This panino is the invention of a friend of mine, Fabien. It creates a complexity of flavours, combining the acidity of the goat's cheese and the elegant sweetness of the pink salami with the spiciness of the mustard.

PINK SALAMI

ZUCCHINI AND SAFFRON PESTO

50 g/2 oz finely machine-sliced pink salami
2 heaped dessertspoons zucchini and saffron pesto

Cut the bread roll in two halves and warm for a few minutes in the oven. Remove from the oven and spread the pesto on one half, topping with the pink salami. Close.

Pink salami is delicate and perfumed: combining it with a spice is an exercise in delicateness because exactly the right balance must be found which allows the flavour to come to the fore without dominating. Saffron is perfect: it helps the rather "shy" pink salami to develop its aromas, despite being without spices itself.

PINK SALAMI

CARCIUGA

50 g/2 oz very finely machine-sliced pink
   salami
2 dessertspoons carciuga (see p. 143)

Divide the bread roll in two and warm it open
in the oven. Then spread one half with the
carciuga and top with the slices of pink salami.
As you close the panino, push down lightly.

*Here, the artichoke is the joint protagonist of
the panino: its vegetable element alongside the
richness of the extra-virgin olive oil combines
well with the delicateness of the pink salami.
The result is a really tasty panino.*

PINK SALAMI

PECORINO CHEESE WITH SAFFRON

50 g/2 oz finely sliced pink salami

40 g/just under 2 oz pecorino cheese with saffron, cut into two slices of medium thickness

Cut the bread roll in half. Place the slices of pecorino on one half and warm everything briefly in the oven ensuring that the cheese doesn't melt. Once removed from the oven, add the machine-sliced pink salami and close.

Here, we add a spice that heightens the flavour of the salami, with cheese, revisiting a truly classic combination. If you fancy it, a little pepper mustard also goes very well and adds a lovely touch of colour.

DARÌO

50 g/2 oz Valtellina bresaola
40 g/just under 2 oz shavings of reggiano
   parmesan (matured 24 months)
3-4 baby plum tomatoes
A drizzle of extra-virgin olive oil

Divide the bread roll in two halves, warm in
the oven and moisten one half with the extra-
virgin olive oil. Add the finely sliced bresaola
and top with the parmesan shavings and the
sliced tomatoes. Press down lightly as you
close the roll.

BRESAOLA

PARMESAN
AND TOMATO

*This is the panino version of
the "health-conscious" dish par
excellence: bresaola, parmesan
shavings and rocket. Tomatoes
replace the rocket to give it a
fresh vegetable note.*

50 g/2 oz bresaola Valtellina, finely sliced
1 heaped dessertspoon cow's milk robiola cheese
1 layer of grilled marinated zucchini

Cut the bread roll in two and warm both halves in the oven. Spread the robiola on one half, add the zucchini in one layer and top with the finely machine-sliced bresaola.

Here is another panino that allows the health-conscious to eat with great satisfaction!

BRESAOLA

ROBIOLA CHEESE AND ZUCCHINI

GIANNI

50 g/2 oz hand-cut finocchiona
    (see p. 122)
40 g/just under 2 oz medium
    mature pecorino cheese from
    Maremma

Cut the bread roll in half and warm briefly in the oven. Remove and place two slices (about 0.5cm/0.2″ thick) of hand-cut finocchiona salami. Top with the slices of pecorino. The pecorino should be mature but still soft. Close.

This is the absolute classic of all classics, at least in Tuscany, the real difference being the quality of the ingredients.

MARCO

FINOCCHIONA

MATURE PECORINO CHEESE

FINOCCHIONA

HERBED PECORINO CHEESE AND PEPPER MUSTARD

50 g/2 oz finocchiona
40 g/just under 2 oz pecorino cheese with
aromatic herbs, in two slices
1 dessertspoon pepper mustard

For this super-Tuscan panino you could use ciabatta bread or two slices of unsalted Tuscan bread. Proceed in the usual way: cut the ciabatta bread (if using) in two and warm the bread in the oven for few minutes. Place the slices of cheese neatly on one half. Add the mustard and top with the slices of finocchiona, then close.

'Ino's panini don't actually have their own names, but in our workplace lingo they often assume nicknames. The idea of a truly Tuscan panino came about while working on the book "Tuscan Cuisine", and this panino will always be nicknamed "Ale".

MORTADELLA DI PRATO

TURNIP TOPS

50 g/2 oz mortadella from Prato
40 g/just under 2 oz turnip tops

Cut the ciabatta in half and warm it in the oven for a few minutes. Fill it with the machine-sliced mortadella from Prato and complete with the turnip tops.

The turnip tops complement and heighten the spicy and sweet characteristics of the mortadella. If you want to go over the top and you have the ingredients available, you could add a slice of raw milk pecorino from Calvana. This is an area in the Apennine mountains between the provinces of Prato and Florence.

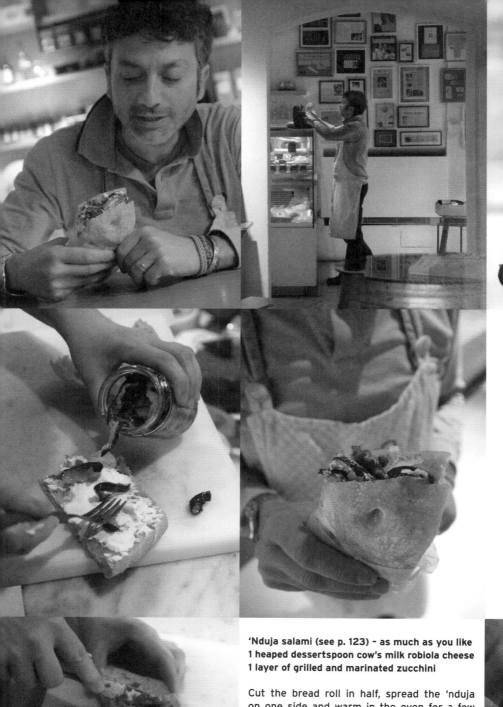

'NDUJA SALAMI

ROBIOLA CHEESE AND ZUCCHINI

'Nduja salami (see p. 123) - as much as you like
1 heaped dessertspoon cow's milk robiola cheese
1 layer of grilled and marinated zucchini

Cut the bread roll in half, spread the 'nduja on one side and warm in the oven for a few minutes. Then cover the other half of the bread with the robiola, top with zucchini and close.

This panino developed from a casual tasting of a roulade with zucchini and 'nduja: the flavours worked well together and it was transformed into a panino. All it needed was a leading element to aid its transformation; robiola cheese is just the thing. It provides acidity, combines the ingredients and moistens the bread.

'NDUJA SALAMI

GORGONZOLA

1 dessertspoon 'nduja salami
2 dessertspoons sweet extra-soft gorgonzola

Cut the ciabatta: on one half, spread the spoonful of 'nduja; on the other half, spread a thick layer of gorgonzola. Warm both halves for a few minutes then close. All the ingredients are warmed to encourage amalgamation: the result is just like a cream!

There are two ingredients in this panino that you wouldn't usually imagine together. Each one is a great protagonist in its own way: the aromatic sweetness of the gorgonzola melts into the spicy savoury richness of the 'nduja.

LEONARDO

BORZILLO

RED EGGPLANT AND SMOKED CACIOCAVALLO CHEESE

50 g/2 oz borzillo salami, cut into regular slices
8-10 small slices of red eggplant from Rotonda in oil
40g/just under 2 oz smoked caciocavallo cheese

Cut the bread roll in two. On one half, spread the cheese that you've cut uniformly but not too thickly. Pop in the oven for a few minutes so that the cheese softens. Once out of the oven, place the eggplant slices directly on top of the caciocavallo, then add the slices of borzillo. Close.

Borzillo is a salami made with the meat of the wild boar. Following an old recipe from Lucca, crunchy Senise peppers are added to the salami mixture. The red eggplant from Rotonda is a very unusual variety of eggplant that can be recognised by its orange skin with beautiful red and green stripes. These make it appear more of a tomato than an eggplant. It is produced in the Valle del Mercure in the province of Potenza, and is a certified Slow Food product; it has a fleshy pulp, a fruity aroma and a very unique flavour that goes wonderfully well with the richness of the borzillo.

vegetarian

SMOKED CACIOCAVALLO CHEESE

TURNIP TOPS

60 g/just over 2 oz smoked caciocavallo
   cheese, cut into two slices
2 dessertspoons turnip tops

Cut the bread roll and place the two slices of
caciocavallo on one half. Pop everything in the
oven to warm. Remove from the oven and add
the turnip tops that you've previously chopped
to ensure an easy bite, then pan-fried in extra-
virgin olive oil, garlic and chilli pepper. Close.

*This is the winter version of the panino with
caciocavallo, eggplant and zucchini on p. 72,
but the result is quite different in texture and
flavour.*

CECILIA

60 g/just over 2 oz smoked caciocavallo cheese
Grilled and marinated eggplant and zucchini in extra-virgin
   olive oil

SMOKED CACIOCAVALLO CHEESE

EGGPLANT AND ZUCCHINI

Cut the bread roll in two. On one half, place the medium slices of caciocavallo cheese, and put everything in the oven for a few minutes. Remove from the oven and top with the grilled and marinated vegetables: put in as many as you like but make sure they are not cold or straight from the fridge!

This is a vegetarian panino par excellence. It came about from the desire to create a recipe with a complexity of flavours without adding fish or meat. The special characteristics of the cheese make this possible. The vegetables add a good crunch to the panino and mingle perfectly with the smokiness of the cheese.

50 g/2 oz fresh Maremma
    pecorino cheese
2 dessertspoons carciuga (see
    p. 143)

Cut the ciabatta in two. On one
half place the thickly sliced
pecorino and put everything in
the oven for a few minutes so
that the cheese softens without
cooking. Remove from the oven
and spread the carciuga on the
other half. Close.

*Here the carciuga is the real star.
The pecorino is a supporting act,
helping to bring out the full glory
of this sauce.*

PECORINO CHEESE

CARCIUGA

HIROKO

PECORINO CHEESE WITH PESTO

TAPENADE AND DRIED TOMATOES

**50 g/2 oz pecorino cheese
with pesto
1 dessertspoon tapenade
10-12 dried Pantelleria tomatoes
in oil**

Cut the bread. On one half place the thickly cut pecorino and pop in the oven for a few minutes. Remove and spread the tapenade on the empty half. Top the cheese with strips of tomato and close.

This is a Mediterranean panino that does just fine without salami. Fresh and aromatic, it has a very full taste.

CRISTINA

PECORINO CHEESE WITH SAFFRON

ZUCCHINI AND PEPPER MUSTARD

50 g/2 oz pecorino cheese with saffron
6-8 slices of grilled marinated zucchini
1 dessertspoon pepper mustard

Cut the bread roll in two. On one half place the pecorino and put everything in the oven for a few minutes. Remove from the oven and spread the mustard over the cheese, top with the zucchini and close.

This is a wonderful panino with beautiful colours: the bright yellow of the pecorino, the red of the mustard and the lustrous veining of the zucchini. It has lovely aromas; when you bite into it, an explosion of sweet, spicy and savoury flavours excites the senses. We suspect that it has aphrodisiac properties.

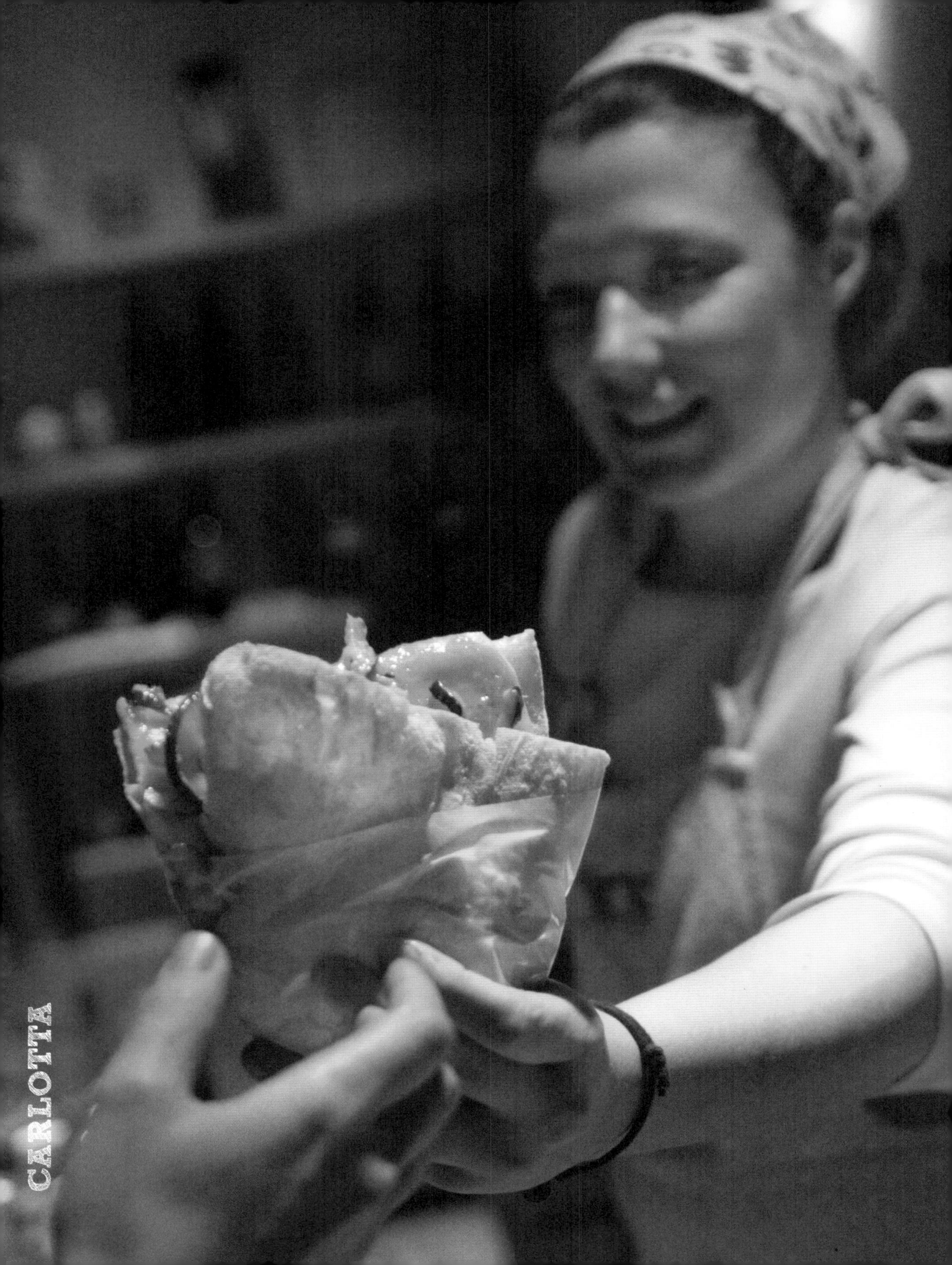
CARLOTTA

CROSTINO WITH ROBIOLA CHEESE

ZUCCHINI AND SAFFRON PESTO

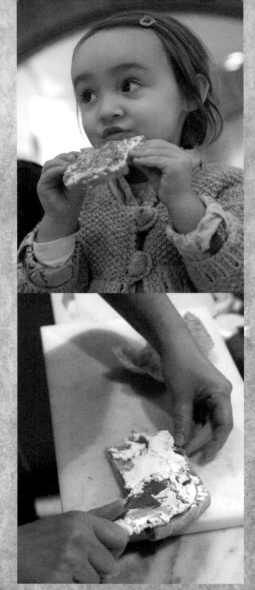

1 scant dessertspoon robiola cheese made with
  cow's milk
2 teaspoons zucchini and saffron pesto

Gently warm a slice of Tuscan bread. Spread it
with robiola and top with a thin layer of pesto.

*This is a children's version. A lot of children
come to 'ino with teeth that are not quite ready
for the thickness of ciabatta; this formula makes
everything easier.*

BIANCA

ROBIOLA CHEESE

ONION PRESERVE

2 dessertspoons robiola cheese made with goat's milk
2 dessertspoons onion preserve

Cut the bread roll in half and warm it for a few minutes. Spread one half with a generous layer of robiola, top with onion preserve and close.

This all began as a dish with sharp robiola cheese in chestnut leaves accompanied perfectly by onion preserve. Why not make a sandwich version?

PARMESAN

TRUFFLE SAUCE

60 g/just over 2 oz reggiano parmesan (matured 24 months)
1 dessertspoon truffle sauce

Split the bread roll in half. Spread the parmesan shavings on one half and warm in the oven for a couple of minutes, taking care not to leave it to cook (the shavings should begin to fuse without changing colour). Remove from the oven and spread the other half with the truffle sauce. Close.

This is the best partner for truffles: a deeply satisfying relationship!

DANIELA

MOZZARELLA CHEESE

BABY PLUM TOMATOES CAPERS AND OREGANO

3-4 slices of Paestum buffalo mozzarella cheese
4 baby plum tomatoes
A drizzle of extra-virgin olive oil
A handful of Pantelleria salted capers
Pantelleria dried oregano (optional)

Cut the bread roll and pop it in the oven. Once out of the oven, spread the drained mozzarella slices on one half and add the finely sliced baby plum tomatoes, the de-salted capers, a drizzle of extra-virgin olive oil and, if you so wish, a sprinkling of oregano.

This is a "caprese" panino-style, but we would never ever call it by this name!

3-4 slices of Paestum buffalo mozzarella cheese
3 dessertspoons friggione (see p. 141)
A handful of Pantelleria dried oregano

Cut the bread roll, briefly warm it and spread the friggione at room temperature (not straight from the fridge!) on one half. Top with the mozzarella cut as you prefer. Complete with a sprinkling of oregano and close.

This panino started out as a game and a bit of provocation; on our menu we called it "our pizza panino". We certainly don't take it seriously, it's only a light-hearted joke, a bit like putting onion in a pummarola sauce...

MOZZARELLA CHEESE

FRIGGIONE

BURRATA STRIPS
DRIED TOMATOES
AND OREGANO

3 strips of burrata
3 dried tomatoes in oil
A thin drizzle of extra-virgin olive oil
A handful of Pantelleria dried
     oregano

Cut the bread roll and warm it in
the oven for a couple of minutes.
Remove from the oven and place a
generous layer of burrata strips on
one half. Add the dried tomatoes, a
little extra-virgin olive oil and finally
the oregano.
If you like them, you could also add
capers.

*This panino came from a yearning
for the sea: this panino is perfect for
eating there!*

from the sea

MACKEREL

ROBIOLA CHEESE AND ZUCCHINI

80 g/just under 3 oz mackerel fillets in oil
1 dessertspoon robiola cheese made with cow's milk
4-5 grilled marinated zucchini in extra-virgin olive oil

In a bowl, finely chop the mackerel fillets. Mix them with the robiola and the chopped zucchini. When the mixture is smooth, spread it on warm bread.

This panino recalls the Sicilian tradition of bringing together fish and cheese. The addition of a slightly acidic vegetable element creates a contrast with the richness of the fish and gives a crunchy texture.

BARBARA

TUNA FILLETS

CARCIUGA
AND OREGANO

80 g/just under 3 oz tuna fillets in oil
    (the best you can find)
1 dessertspoon carciuga (see p. 143)
Pantelleria dried oregano

Cut the bread in half and warm it for a few minutes. Spread the carciuga on one half, top with the crumbled tuna fillets and complete with a sprinkling of oregano.

The idea began with combining tuna and artichokes, but the addition of carciuga makes the whole thing more original. It has a real hint of the sea about it. The panino is completed by adding a touch of oregano.

A MEMORY OF CETARA

TUNA

DRIED TOMATOES, SCAROLA LETTUCE, CAPERS AND ANCHOVY OIL

80 g/just under 3 oz tuna fillets
4-5 dried tomatoes in oil
A few scarola lettuce leaves
A few drops of Cetara anchovy soaking oil
A handful of de-salted Pantelleria capers

Cut the ciabatta in half and warm it briefly in the oven. Prepare a "salad" separately (ideally in advance so that it can marinate a little) of crumbled tuna fillets, chopped scarola lettuce, de-salted capers, dried tomatoes, anchovy soaking oil and extra-virgin olive oil (no salt is needed!). Fill the warm ciabatta with a generous helping of "salad" and close.

This started out as a dish from Cetara eaten by Pasquale Torrente; the memory of it was transformed into a panino.

SMOKED SALTED COD'S LIVER

TURNIP TOPS

60 g/just over 2 oz smoked salted cod's liver
3 dessertspoons pan-fried turnip tops

Cut the bread roll in half and warm it for a few minutes. Remove from the oven. First, place the salted cod's liver on one half, followed by the turnip tops which you have previously cooked and cut into pieces. If you wish to go overboard, you can spread the bread with a layer of salted butter.

Cod's liver brings to mind foie gras: it has a similar texture and richness and the flavour comes pretty close, too. The bitter acidic notes of the turnip tops help to tone down the sweet richness of the liver.

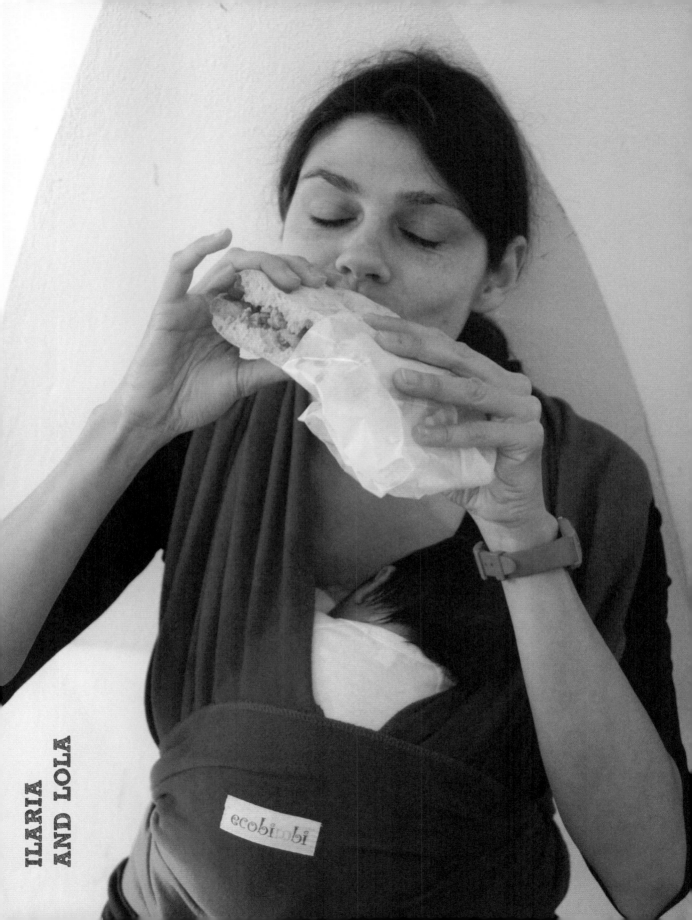

ILARIA
AND LOLA

60 g salmerino (char)
A handful of juniper berries
A few drops of dwarf pine oil
20 g/just under 1 oz alpine butter
Savory
Black bread

Cut the black bread into neat slices and spread them with butter. Place the char fish slices on the top. Add a drop or two of dwarf pine oil, a sprinkling of savory, a handful of juniper berries and a pinch of black pepper.

SALMERINO

JUNIPER, DWARF PINE OIL AND SAVORY

This panino reminds of Trentino, and its products. The salmerino, or char, is a freshwater fish characterised by its ability to live only in extremely cold clear water. It has existed since ancient times and is considered almost a relic of the ice age. It is similar to the trout, but its flesh is more delicate and compact. Its fillets are first salted by hand and then smoked in alpine wood. Dwarf pine oil is an essential oil extracted from the branches of the dwarf pine tree. Together with juniper, it enhances the alpine flavour.

ANCHOVIES

ROBIOLA CHEESE

5 Cetara anchovies
60 g/just over 2 oz robiola cheese made with Roccaverano
** or Piedmont goat's milk**

Cut the bread roll in half and put it in the oven just long enough for it to warm. Spread the robiola on one half, top with the anchovies and close.

This is a cousin of the irreplaceable bread, butter and anchovy panino.
You must try it.

ANCHOVIES

PEPPERS AND TAPENADE

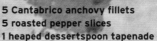

5 Cantabrico anchovy fillets
5 roasted pepper slices
1 heaped dessertspoon tapenade

Warm the cut bread for a few minutes then spread the tapenade on one half. Top with the peppers and complete with the very special Cantabrico anchovies. Close.

This is a rather unusual panino that is delicious without salami or cheese. The inspiration for it came from Spanish tapas, in which you can often find anchovies and peppers together. In the panino version, tapenade is added because the extra-virgin olive oil it contains helps the flavours to mature and its creaminess completes the whole effect.

ANCHOVIES

SCAMORZA CHEESE

4 Mediterranean anchovy fillets
60 g/just over 2 oz scamorza cheese
A small quantity of dried Pantelleria oregano
   as desired

Cut the bread in two. On one half place a thick slice of scamorza and pop everything in the oven for a couple of minutes. Remove from the oven and add the anchovies, without draining away all the oil; leave a little to soak into the bread and cheese. If you so wish, you can sprinkle with oregano, then close.

A combination of land and sea, this panino brings a simple cheese with a milky aftertaste together with the salty flavour of the anchovies. It is a classic example of how you can create a perfect union of flavours using only two quite basic ingredients.

MOZZARELLA CHEESE AND ANCHOVY OIL

5-6 fillets Cetara anchovies
2-3 slices of Paestum buffalo mozzarella
    cheese
A few drops of Cetara anchovy soaking oil
A pinch of dried Pantelleria oregano

Cut the bread roll and warm the two halves in the oven. Remove from the oven and place the mozzarella on one half, drizzle a few drops of anchovy oil on the top and add the anchovy fillets with a pinch of oregano. Close the panino and press down lightly.

This is one of the most extraordinary combinations that nature has to offer; instant excitement that leaves you speechless. Just close your eyes and bite into it!

CLAIRE

ANCHOVIES

BUFFALO RICOTTA CHEESE, DRIED TOMATOES, CAPERS, OREGANO AND ANCHOVY OIL

I LOVE THE SOUTH

4 Cetara anchovies
2 dessertspoons buffalo ricotta cheese
3 dried tomatoes in oil
A handful of salted Pantelleria capers
A sprinkling of dried Pantelleria oregano
A few drops of Cetara anchovy soaking oil

Cut the bread, warm both halves in the oven for a few minutes then spread the ricotta on one half. Add the sliced dried tomatoes, the anchovies and the capers. Top with the oregano and the anchovy soaking oil then close.

Ricotta makes a great base for enhancing the Mediterranean aromas of sun and sea.

FRANCESCA

5 Cetara anchovy fillets
2 dessertspoons burrata strips
The zest of an untreated lemon

Cut the bread in half, warm it in the oven and place the burrata strips on one half. Remove from the oven and top with the anchovy fillets. Complete with plenty of freshly grated untreated lemon zest. Close it and enjoy!

The grated lemon zest makes all the difference in this panino. It releases the aromas and binds all the ingredients together.

ANCHOVIES

BURRATA STRIPS
AND LEMON ZEST

5 Cetara anchovy fillets
1 scoop (approx. 50 g/2 oz) sweet gorgonzola

Cut the bread in two. Spread the gorgonzola on one half and pop everything in the oven for a few minutes. Remove from the oven and add the anchovies. Close.

An unusual classic.

ANCHOVIES

GORGONZOLA

BREAD
BUTTER AND
ANCHOVIES

Good butter
Cetara anchovy fillets
Tuscan bread

Cut the Tuscan bread into thin slices and toast them well. Spread with butter and top with the anchovies.
This recipe doesn't need quantities.

This is the quintessence of simplicity and satisfaction! You can eat this any time of day: when you wake up, for lunch, as an afternoon snack and even before going to bed.

ingredients

  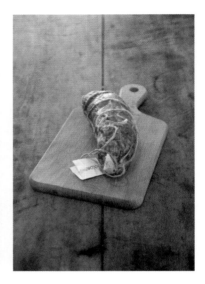

TUSCAN CURED HAM

In Tuscany, cured ham has various degrees of quality and there are many different ways of producing it, but its most important characteristic is saltiness, which can sometimes be excessive. For this reason, it's important to use ham that doesn't have too much salt, otherwise it can be invasive. It's much better to buy ham that has been matured for about 24 months. It is important to machine-slice it very thinly.

TUSCAN SALAMI

As far as salami in Tuscany and other regions is concerned, every province and area has its own recipe; every butcher also has a recipe of his own. The type of grain varies, as well as the quality of fat used and the maturing time. The use of spices is paramount; every formula is unique and, naturally, top secret.

A salami that is not too spicy and allows for combinations with other ingredients is recommended. The degree of softness is also important: if a salami is too hard, the bite is unpleasant. For this same reason, the salami should be cut by hand into slices that are not too thick.

FINOCCHIONA

Perhaps the most famous among Tuscan salamis, the finocchiona is a sausage made with pork meat and seasoned with garlic and, above all, fennel seeds that give the salami its name. Fennel seeds had been used in the past for their aromatic properties, as they were ideal for disguising the smell and taste of lower quality meat.

It is a highly popular salami in Tuscany. You can find it in two different sizes: the first is wide; the second much narrower in diameter (this is used for 'ino's paninos) that makes it similar to the shape of salami, even if slightly bigger. Compared to other salamis, finocchiona is softer, fresher and tends to crumble when cut.

It should be cut with a knife. Being such a flavoursome salami, it goes very well with various types of pecorino cheese as well as pepper mustard.

TUSCAN CURED HAM   TUSCAN SALAMI   FINOCCHIONA

BRESAOLA MORTADELLA 'NDUJA SALAMI

BRESAOLA

This is a rare example of a salami without pork meat: the Valtellina bresaola is made using beef (mainly topside or round). A process of salting, drying and maturing is followed which can take between 2 and 24 months. Bresaola has been produced for centuries in the two valleys of the province of Sondrio, Valtellina and Valchiavenna, using recipes handed down through generations initially for home consumption and then to be sold. It is a lean, guilt-free ingredient that allows even the most health-conscious to savour the soft texture and delicious taste of salami in their panini.
It should be machine-cut very thinly.

TRADITIONAL BOLOGNA MORTADELLA

The most famous and loved mortadella for its aroma, texture and flavour, Bologna Mortadella is a cooked salami with a noble and ancient history. It is made using selected cuts of pork meat that are chopped in various ways until a very fine mixture is achieved. Small cubes of fat are added, which are exclusively taken from the adipose tissue of the pig's throat. The mortadella is then cooked in special dry wood burning ovens following strict timing and procedures.
It should be neatly and very thinly machine-cut; it will happily accompany many different flavours, from parmesan to gorgonzola, from mustard to peppers with truffles.

'NDUJA SALAMI

This is a traditional salami from Calabria with a soft, almost spreadable texture, traditionally produced in the area of Vibo Valentia, around Monte Poro and Spilinga. The abundance of chilli peppers mixed with the pork meats and fats gives it a bright red colour. It is stuffed into its own natural casing, lightly smoked then matured. It has a strong spicy taste that demands the accompaniment of sweeter elements. Being spreadable, it literally manages to melt, almost like a sauce.

PINK SALAMI

This is a very unusual salami with an ancient tradition. Today it has almost been forgotten. It was originally prepared with a knife, using all the best parts of the pig. The few existing producers of pink salami use, as tradition dictates, selected lean (thigh and shoulder) and fatty (exclusively guanciale or cheek) cuts of pork.

As with traditional Bologna mortadella, which is similar, pink salami is cooked in wood burning ovens with scrupulous attention to cooking temperatures: excessive cooking risks dispersion of precious aromas and flavours.

It is a great substitute for cooked ham. It should be cut quite finely with a meat slicer.

PINK SALAMI

MORTADELLA DI PRATO

This cooked salami is special because of its strong distinct spices, which include cinnamon, cloves, coriander, black pepper, mace and, above all, the liqueur Alchermes that adds colour and a pronounced note of sweetness.

Typically produced in the area of Prato since the beginning of the 1900s, this mortadella was forgotten for a while in the post-war period, probably because it was considered a humble, rather rustic salami. Recently rediscovered and revalued, mortadella di Prato has become a certified Slow Food product thanks to perfected production techniques in terms of hot packaging, the selection of meats and the quantity/quality of spices used.

It is a strong ingredient with exquisite aromas and sweet to the taste. It should be thinly cut using a meat slicer.

MORTADELLA DI PRATO

FRESH PECORINO CHEESE

This is a sweet, slow-matured cheese from the Maremma area. It retains a soft, almost runny, texture that has a tendency to stick to the knife when cut.
Its main quality is a sweet milky taste that complements and enhances the strength of the other ingredients, including, for example, carciuga.

MATURE PECORINO CHEESE

Behind these two words lies an entire universe of flavours and textures.
At 'ino, we use a pecorino from the Maremma area, mature but still soft; full of flavour but a long way from the hard, dry texture that would make it difficult to add to a panino.

PECORINO CHEESE WITH AROMATIC HERBS

This is a fresh pecorino covered in extra-virgin olive oil and then passed through chopped aromatic herbs (sage, mint, savory, basil, rosemary and coriander). This forms a delicious crust that allows the mixture of flavours to permeate the cheese. It is a real pleasure to eat.

PECORINO CHEESE FRESH MATURE WITH HERBS

PECORINO CHEESE WITH PESTO

This is a fresh pecorino with San Rossore pine nuts and the celebrated Pra' basil added. It recreates the content and aroma of pesto but with a milky base.
A fun ingredient, it allows us to play with Mediterranean combinations of olives, dried tomatoes and extra-virgin olive oil.

PECORINO CHEESE WITH PISTACHIO NUTS

This is a fresh pecorino with a large quantity of Bronte pistachios added. The cheese is compact but still extremely soft and milky white in colour. It has an unexpected element of dried fruit in its sweet taste as well as in its texture.

PECORINO CHEESE WITH SAFFRON

This is a medium-mature pecorino produced with milk from the Crete Senesi area of Tuscany. Several saffron threads are added to the milk, to infuse. Saffron from Tuscany is used, which is produced in traditional ways in San Gimignano, San Polo and other areas of the region.
This type of pecorino develops a lovely fragrance of saffron that has great intensity and character.

WITH PESTO PISTACHIO SAFFRON

BUFFALO MOZZARELLA CHEESE

A fresh stretched cheese produced using buffalo milk, buffalo mozzarella is well known by name even if it is not always produced with the necessary care to ensure high standards, therefore it is important to choose a quality buffalo mozzarella, paying close attention to its origin. At 'ino, we use buffalo mozzarella campana, which comes from the Paestum (Capaccio) area, in large 500g/17oz pieces.

Once bought, the mozzarella should be kept in its own whey, covered and out of the fridge in a cool place. When you are ready to use it, cut it into large slices (at least 1cm/just under half an inch thick), then drain it; if you wish to really appreciate its wonderful texture and inestimable taste, don't heat it.

BUFFALO MOZZARELLA CHEESE

 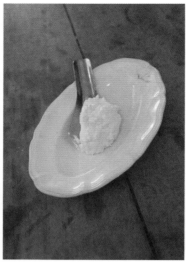 

BUTTER

Get the best you can!

RICOTTA CHEESE

For 'ino's panini we use buffalo and sheep's milk ricotta.
When choosing this apparently modest ingredient it is fundamental to check it is really fresh so as to fully enjoy all its delicate aromas. Ricotta, despite having a decisive flavour of its own, doesn't overwhelm other ingredients in the panino, but gently gathers and binds them together.

BURRATA STRIPS

Also known as *stracciatella*, this is the particular mozzarella mixture (made with buffalo or cow's milk), that is stretched by hand, mixed with cream and forms the filling of the burrata. It is a typical traditional product of Puglia, especially Murgia (in the provinces of Barletta-Andria-Trani and Bari).
It has a sweet flavour and a pliant texture and is certainly one of the most lustful ingredients you can find!

BUTTER   RICOTTA CHEESE   BURRATA STRIPS

ROBIOLA CHEESE SCAMORZA CHEESE PARMESAN

ROBIOLA CHEESE

A cheese with a soft texture, robiola can be produced using cow's, goat's or sheep's milk, or indeed a mix of varying percentages of different milk types. It has a fresh flavour and good acidity, which is obviously more pronounced in the goat's milk version.

In a panino, it has the fundamental roles of creating softness and binding the different ingredients together, a kind of "anchor" for all the flavours.

SCAMORZA CHEESE

This is made of cow's milk and is typical of the central southern area of Italy. It can be produced in different shapes with various degrees of maturing. At 'ino, we use the typical torpedo shape that is still fresh. Characterised by a strong milky scent, it is lovely when gently warmed as it literally brings all the other ingredients together.

PARMESAN

Parmigiano (parmesan) reggiano is a miracle of perfection, a unique cheese that has been produced in the same way for nine centuries. Extremely digestible, healthy and tasty, it can be used for both simple and sophisticated combinations. For 'ino's panini, we choose a parmigiano reggiano that has been matured for 24 months. Medium-sized shavings are gently warmed just enough for them to soften without colouring or cooking.

SMOKED CACIOCAVALLO CHEESE

This is a smoked cheese made of buffalo and cow's milk. It comes from the Sele plains in Capaccio, in the province of Salerno. It has an intense flavour and extraordinary aromas that come from the richness of the milk, but also from the strong smokiness perceptible in both scent and aspect: it has a beautiful toasted colour.

It should be heated in a panino because its fullness allows it to soften without melting, leaving an explosion of flavour and taste in the mouth that isn't at all invasive.
It goes very well with mortadella, but also with the aromatic quality of turnip tops and most other vegetables.

SMOKED CACIOCAVALLO CHEESE

GORGONZOLA

Produced in Lombardy and the province of Novara for centuries, this is without doubt the most well known Italian blue-veined cheese. It is made using cow's milk with added enzymes and selected moulds. It comes in large forms of 12kg/just over 26lb and, according to how long it has been matured, it can be sweet (2 months) or spicy (over 3 months).

At 'ino, we use sweet gorgonzola: its runny, highly aromatic consistency softens the composition of the panino and binds its sweet notes with ingredients that are strong in taste and spiciness.
The idea of combining it with anchovies is both interesting and unusual.

GORGONZOLA

CARCIOFI ALLA CAFONA

These are whole Roman artichokes, blanched and preserved in extra-virgin olive oil with a few added spices. The special characteristic of carciofi alla cafona is, besides its taste, an extraordinary crunchiness that is delicious in a panino, with salami and cheese.

BABY PLUM TOMATOES

These tomatoes are very small, deep red and extremely sweet. Their Italian name, "datterini", comes from their elongated shape similar to a date. They have a delicate skin and so are perfect for eating raw.

CARCIOFI ALLA CAFONA BABY PLUM TOMATOES

ANCHOVIES

Mediterranean, Cetara and Cantabrico anchovies are an extremely precious ingredient for panini. A concentration of taste and sea that successfully links complex ingredients in surprising combinations (such as salami and truffles), but also in simple duos.

CETARA ANCHOVY OIL

This is none other than the liquid obtained from the infusion of gutted anchovies in salt, the sea concentrated in one special oil. Cetara anchovies are fished during a set period (from March to July), gutted then placed in a salt solution for a day. They are then transferred to wooden containers similar to small barrels and placed in alternating layers of salt. A weight is placed on the top of each barrel that, as it pushes down on the fish, favours the elimination of water. The liquid that comes from this process is collected and exposed to sunlight for several months, and then put back into the anchovy preserving barrels. It is then filtered. A kind of "sea juice", it is used with a dropper to add a very intense aroma to food.

MACKEREL

A freshwater fish with excellent nutritional qualities, mackerel has always been one of the most preserved seafoods. The presence of Omega-3 makes this a healthy fatty fish. It has tasty yet delicate flesh. The fillets used at 'ino are from Cetara. They are blanched and preserved in oil; just before completing a panino, they are drained and chopped.

ANCHOVIES CETARA ANCHOVY OIL MACKEREL

FRIGGIONE

This is a so-called "fake" sauce from Emilia Romagna: an exclusively vegetarian ragù with tomatoes, onions and extra-virgin olive oil. The secret of its flavour lies not only in the quality of ingredients used but also in slow, patient cooking; traditionally, the sauce would remain in the pan on the edge of the stove from morning to evening while the farm work was being done.

It goes very well in a panino: it softens the consistency and introduces an acidic vegetable note with the tomatoes. This is a playful take on traditional flavour combinations, using, for example, mozzarella.

FRIGGIONE

CARCIUGA

As its Italian name suggests, this is a pâté of artichokes and anchovies (carciofo + acciuga), in which the artichokes are left in deliberately large pieces while the anchovies are completely melted. This combination is emulsified with high quality extra-virgin olive oil.

This sauce shows just how well the sweetness of the artichokes goes with the strong savoury flavour of the anchovies.

Using the bread as a mediator, carciuga also combines well with ingredients such as pink salami and pecorino; you can afford to use as much of it as you like as it is a delicate and well-balanced sauce.

CARCIUGA

PEPPER MUSTARD

Sweet and aromatic, with a slightly spicy note, this sauce is made using red peppers and has the consistency of a glaze. Its taste is so unusual that it binds itself to important and sometimes heavier ingredients such as gorgonzola and mortadella, introducing a hint of spice.

The ideal way to add it to a panino it to use a squeezable bottle, drawing a zig-zag all over the surface, so as not to overdo the quantity and to make sure you spread it uniformly.

PEPPER MUSTARD

PARMESAN CREAM

Who says there isn't a spreadable cheese that is exciting?

PARMESAN CREAM

ZUCCHINI AND SAFFRON PESTO

This is a cream made by grinding zucchini in plenty of extra-virgin olive oil with saffron threads. It is an absolute treat for vegetarians!

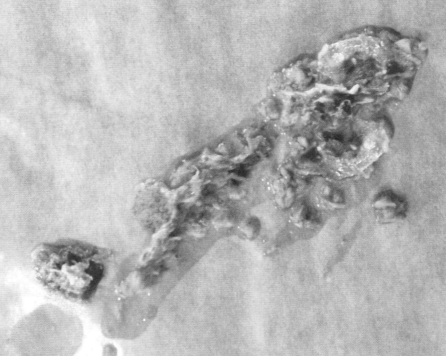

ZUCCHINI AND SAFFRON PESTO

TRUFFLE SAUCE

Truffles are sheer fragrance. In a panino, a sauce is used out of necessity due to the limited availability and cost of truffles, but also because it has the dual task of moistening the bread and binding the ingredients together. The sauce uses white truffles as its base and it keeps all its promises, combining especially well with the richness of the mortadella but also with the well-rounded mature flavour of the parmigiano reggiano.

It should be used sparingly to avoid overwhelming the other elements.

TRUFFLE SAUCE

TAPENADE

TAPENADE

This is a Provençale sauce made from finely chopped black olives, capers and anchovies emulsified with extra-virgin olive oil. It has a persistent and pleasant aroma through which strong vegetable scents of olives and oil emerge, at the same time introducing tangy notes of anchovies and the aromatic properties of the capers.

In a panino, it provides Mediterranean moisture and fragrance. You can use as much as you like, but as it is very flavoursome, be careful not to risk overdoing the saltiness.

TAPENADE

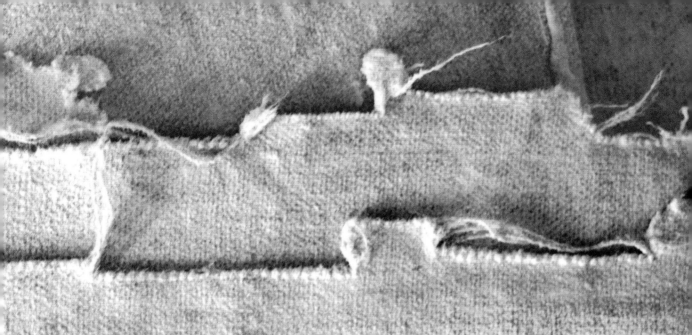

the bakers

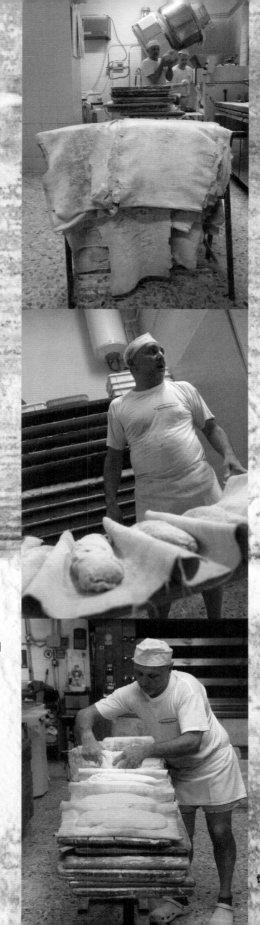

White nights

We arrived by the pink light of sunrise
beside the River Arno, with the
vegetable garden behind the house and
the doorstep dusted with flour.
Stefano and Dimitri were already at
work and hurrying as the yeast won't
wait; there is never enough time to
produce 400kg/14oz in just one night.
At 7.30pm, water is being added,
the yeast assessed; it's important to
calculate exactly the right measures
according to temperature and humidity
levels: if the day had been hot, if
the night is damp and if outside it is
freezing as the bread turns golden.

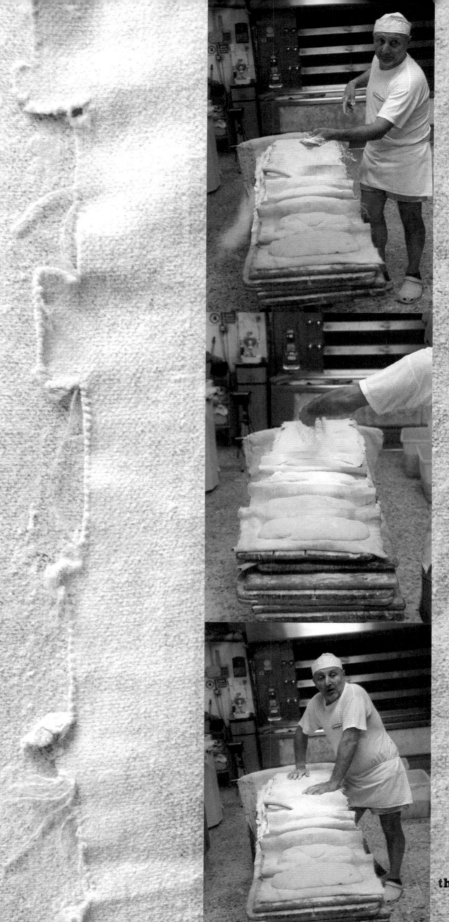

The Cirri brothers are artists who continue the work of their father, grandfather and uncle. Since 1990, they have made the business their own, and do everything themselves, six nights a week even if before it was seven, without a minute's rest.

Although there are modern ovens and machines, the brothers are truly working hard, running back and forth, head, hands and eyes fully occupied. They fix the axes on the mobile shelves, stretch out cloths whitened by flour that seem like art canvases and pass the bread dough like a living thing, making it jump from one hand to another. The movements are always the same, measured with precision and repeated three times every night, and a long, long time before that in this very place.

Pieces of bread encrusted with the night's flour are beautiful and we fall in love with them: they are a delight to photograph, lovely to see and to think that they have always been like this, today just as in the 1400s.

Among the different types of bread made daily, little specialities are created using different processes. Pan di ramerino is one of Florence's glorious examples.

In order to prepare it, Stefano uses the same method as for bread making: type "O" flour, water and starter dough, but to this he adds raisins, sugar, rosemary and extra-virgin olive oil. Lard was used in the original recipe but this has been replaced by plenty of healthier olive oil. The whole dough is left to rise for about twenty minutes, before being taken apart and shaped into panino rolls by hand.

They are left to rise again for the same amount of time. Then they are brushed with egg yolk and scored.
The rolls are left to rest for another 40 minutes and when they have risen enough they are placed in a very hot oven (300°C/570°F) for five to six minutes. Once removed from the oven, they are given a final brushing with a sugar syrup as a tantalising glaze.

PAN DI RAMERINO

'Ino's ciabatta

In reality, the pressured night work already began the previous day. When everything has been baked, the new dough for the following night is prepared. It is picked up again when it is time to start back at work after 12 hours of rising time, and it is fed, fattened with flour and left to rise in a tub for another hour and a half. It is lifted with great strength, soft and alive, and spread out on the work surface, cleared of all previous activity, to rise again. There is a continuous folding, tucking and reining in because it moves and flops over the side.

Finally, it is time to cut it into large pieces and then into smaller ciabatta loaf shapes. They weigh about 300 g/10.5 oz uncooked and will weigh approximately 240g-260g/ 8.5-just over 9oz when baked. Dusted with fresh flour and left to rise for the last time in their final shape, these will become 'ino's bread.

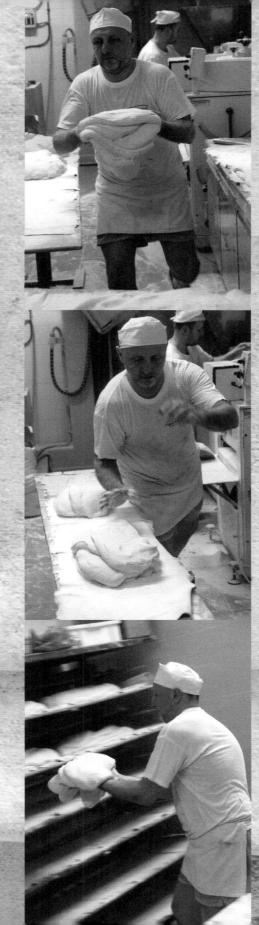

The oven

The mouth of the oven is wide but it's anyone's guess as to how deep it is. Uncooked loaves, small ciabatta and other breads still soft and white, finger imprints on the top, are all lined up like rows of soldiers.

Stefano knows when the time is perfect, when the level of heat is just right, where to begin and where to end, which corner is the hottest and which has just the right warmth. Moving the baker's shovel around he seems like a juggler; he sniffs the air and has a certain natural instinct. He keeps an eye on the time and the scent while he begins to make the new dough again.

Suddenly, the time is right and out comes the bread in a great rush, all golden and striped with flour.

On the shovel, on the surface and in baskets, straight, stiff and proud to be beautiful.

Outside it is still night, but soon it will be morning.

index

classics

vegetarian

from the sea

ingredients

acknowledgments

Thank you.

This book of panini and people has its mouth full of thanks.
First of all, thank you to everyone involved; in strict order of appearance thanks go to: Michele, Catia, Bianca, Silvia, Aldo, Elisabetta, Marco, Carlotta, Giuseppe, Giulia, Alessandro, Duccio, Nidia, Simona, Darío, Gianni, Marco, Leonardo, Cecilia, Hiroko, Cristina, Carlotta, Bianca, Serena, Daniela, Barbara, Maurizio, Ilaria and little Lola, Paola, Fabio, Claire, Francesca and Anna.
Thanks to all those who have worked, and continue to work, on a daily basis, in particular Carlotta, Hiroko and Serena who have borne our presence with infinite patience, even in the most chaotic moments.
Thank you to brothers Stefano and Dimitri Cirri, the wonderful bakers who welcomed us for almost a whole night in their bakery in Scandicci, beside the River Arno.
Sincere thanks go to Guido Tommasi for believing in the project with us.

© Datanova S.r.l. (Guido Tommasi Editore), 2018

Text: Maria Teresa Di Marco, Alessandro Frassica
Photographs: Maurizio Maurizi
Graphics: Maurizio Maurizi, Tommaso Bacciocchi
Translation: Lucy Howell
Editorial: Anita Ravasio

ISBN: 978 88 6753 218 6

Printed in Italy by Printer Trento s.r.l.